STRATEGIC THINKING FOR PLANNING AND EXECUTION

A practical booklet for managers

by

Ken Thompson

October 2018
REVISION: 0.04

STRATEGIC THINKING FOR PLANNING AND EXECUTION
A practical booklet for managers

CONTENTS

- HOW TO USE THIS BOOKLET 3
- SUMMARY INFOGRAPHIC 4
- THE EXAMPLE PROJECT 5
- 1. GOALS & OBJECTIVES 6
- 2. MISSION & VALUES 8
- 3. SOCIAL LANDSCAPE 10
- 4. INFORMATION RESEARCH 12
- 5. FITNESS ASSESSMENT 14
- 6. OBSTACLES & DILEMMAS 16
- 7. KEY PERFORMANCE INDICATORS (KPIs) 17
- 8. CRITICAL SUCCESS FACTORS (CSFs) 19
- 9. STRATEGIC SUMMARY 20
- THE FULL PROCESS ON ONE PAGE 22
- WORKED EXAMPLE 23
- BLANK TEMPLATE 24
- THE SYSTEMATIC GUIDES SERIES 26
- ABOUT THE AUTHOR 27

STRATEGIC THINKING FOR PLANNING AND EXECUTION
A practical booklet for managers

HOW TO USE THIS BOOKLET

> "Mistakes can and should be tolerated, provided one learns from them, but too many mistakes erode confidence, particularly if they are what one company, W.L. Gore, calls below-the-waterline mistakes which imperil the organization." —*Professor Charles Handy*
>
> "Strategy without tactics is the slowest route to victory, tactics without strategy is the noise before defeat." —*Sun Tsu*

Many, if not most, planning errors in projects and ventures of all types and sizes are not usually problems of misinterpretation or misunderstanding of complexity but rather simple errors of omission, unchecked assumptions and careless research due to adopting an unsystematic or ad hoc approach to this important task.

A second equally large problem is the difficulty planners seem to encounter in successfully integrating existing and new strategy into their planning thinking. This often results in plans which are disconnected from the directions, priorities and values of the host enterprise.

This booklet attempts to addresses both problems by providing a systematic approach (based on 30 questions) to defining strategy for immediate use within the planning process.

The booklet provides a nine-step express process (with templates) with each step defined in detail and highlighted using a worked example from personal life which any reader can relate to.

The objective is to enable an individual or team to come up with a **solid "project scoping" which can be used to effectively and strategically direct whatever happens next**, such as execution (small projects) or detailed planning (larger projects). *All in an hour or two rather than a month or two!*

Finally, I have tried to err on the side of brevity and to avoid the temptation to be overly prescriptive as this frequently results in bureaucracy and over-dependency on "the method" at the expense of common sense, ownership and the quality of thinking.

STRATEGIC THINKING FOR PLANNING AND EXECUTION
A practical booklet for managers

SUMMARY INFOGRAPHIC

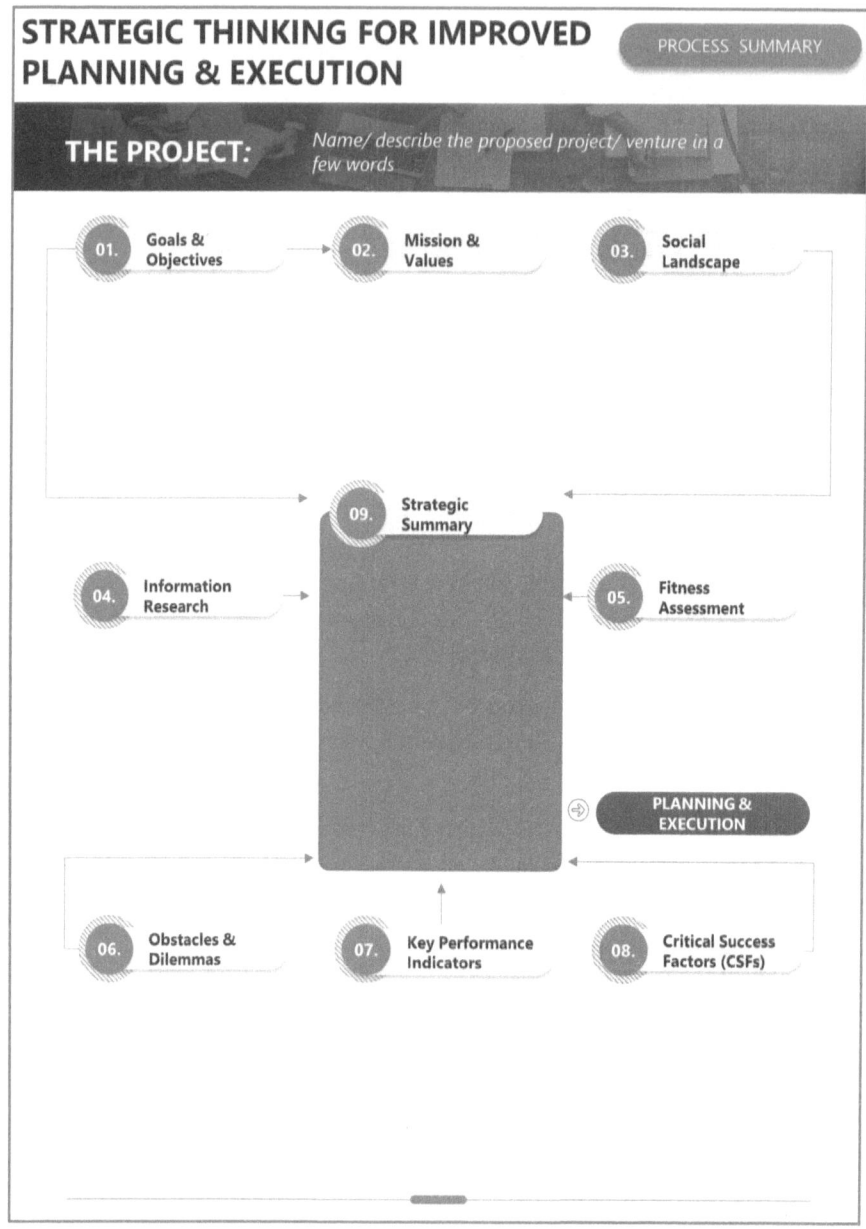

STRATEGIC THINKING FOR PLANNING AND EXECUTION
A practical booklet for managers

THE EXAMPLE PROJECT

> You were out having a coffee with Fred, your friend and neighbour and you both decided that enough was enough! You are both going to take up running and train together each week in preparation for a 5K park run in 3 months.

I will use this project, which most people should be able to identify with, as a simple worked example to illustrate the different steps in the process of quickly developing a sensible and well-thought through high-level project plan using the strategic thinking process described in the booklet.

STRATEGIC THINKING FOR PLANNING AND EXECUTION
A practical booklet for managers

1. GOALS & OBJECTIVES

THE KEY QUESTIONS

- What must be achieved by when and for whom?

PROJECT EXAMPLE: *Couch to 5K with Fred*

Goals/Objectives:
- Work up to being able to run 5K
- with Fred Next Door
- culminating in a Park run in about 3 month's time
- losing half a stone along the way
- whilst doing something a bit competitive
- to improve my health for my own and partners benefit (The Customer)

PROCESS & TOOLS

First I will try and clarify the essential difference between a Goal and an Objective. The simplest distinction I can make is whilst Goals and Objectives are both summary statements of ambition/intent an Objective is timebound and has specific measures of success. Another way to put it is that an Objective has an associated Target but a Goal does not.

Some suggest that you set Goals first and then you set one or many Objectives to support them. Others argue that your Goals evolve into your Objectives once Targets have been added. However the two terms tend to be used very interchangeably, as I will do here, so it is not worth getting hung up on the difference between them.

The "for whom" part of the question is very important as it is really asking who benefits from the achievement of the Objective. In other words, who is the "customer" who will determine if the objective has been achieved and was worth all the effort and investment. The customer (or customers) are often implied or omitted but it is usually good to be explicit about this right at the start. More about this in the Social Landscape section later.

STRATEGIC THINKING FOR PLANNING AND EXECUTION
A practical booklet for managers

In quantifying your Objectives the most popular tool is the *Smart Objective*, attributed to *Peter Drucker*, which suggests that each of your objectives should be:

- Specific
- Measurable
- Achievable
- Relevant
- Time bound

"SMART" is a very useful acronym however three words of caution:

Measurable versus Important

It is usually much easier to make measurable things important than to make important things measurable. **Read this sentence a few times!** Be careful not to prioritise those targets which are easy to measure over those which are more important.

Precision versus Accuracy

Just because something is precise it does not mean it is accurate. The fact my calculator suggests that I can lose *precisely* 7.29 lbs does not mean this is an accurate statement. In initial objective setting I recommend you use broad brush numbers (e.g. half a stone) to make this very clear. You should then refine these as you gain more insight into what your project actually involves and what is realistic. You might notice in the example project I have not yet stated any target for how long it might take me to run the 5K!

Articulating your objectives

There is no right or wrong way to articulate your objectives but I would recommend you start with discrete bullet points and then link them into sentences in the way I have articulated the goals/objectives in the example project. This technique is known as an *Agile Story*. You can then elaborate the narrative as you need to later but confident it is based on a solid set of discrete and clear points. **The other advantage of this approach is you can record your bullet points on the blank planning template (page 24-25) as you go - thus being able to develop and see the whole picture on a single page as in the worked example (page 23).**

STRATEGIC THINKING FOR PLANNING AND EXECUTION
A practical booklet for managers

2. MISSION & VALUES

THE KEY QUESTIONS

- Why should we be doing this project/venture?
- What constraints apply to the way we would do it?

PROJECT EXAMPLE: *Couch to 5K with Fred*

Goals/Objectives:

- Improve Health (Health)
- Career Development (Business)
- New Hobby (Well-being/Active)
- New Friends (Social)
- Stay Healthy (Safety)

PROCESS & TOOLS

Now that you have a specific project in mind you need to take a step back and answer two important questions – *why* would we do this and if so are there any important constraints about *how* we do it. You achieve this by connecting the project to your Mission and your Values.

In theory your Mission and Values should already exist and you are then simply checking how your project Goals/Objectives fit with them. In even purer theory you might have devised your Mission and Values and are now identifying, in a top-down manner, a whole list of projects you wish to consider to execute in support of them. However in practice it is not normally like this – your Mission and Values may not exist on paper or may not be sufficiently developed to cover the areas which your project is potentially addressing.

Like Goals and Objectives we need to clarify what we mean by Mission and Values. Your Mission (or Vision) is a high-level statement about who "you" (Individually or Corporately) are and what is important to you from an enduring perspective. PepsiCo allegedly had a famous Mission Statement which was simply "Beat Coke". Your Values concern your behaviours and what they need to be if you really have such a Mission (identity and priorities) and want to be true to it. *Integrity* is the term given to someone who displays coherence between their Identity and their Behaviours.

When you are constructing your values statement it always pays to remember the French national tripartite motto "Liberté, égalité, fraternité" meaning, of course, liberty, equality and fraternity. Perhaps surprisingly, there are three conflicts, or *dilemmas* as I prefer to call them, already built in to one of the most famous values statement's in the world:

- *Liberty vs Equality*
- *Equality vs Fraternity*
- *Fraternity vs Liberty*

For example, what happens to your Equality when my expression of Liberty results in me having much more than you have? Or when my personal Equality (human rights) overpowers my desire to show Fraternity (brotherhood) when you need my support.

Values should not be designed to make us feel inspired but rather to help us reach difficult personal decisions when we encounter daily operational and strategic dilemmas such as Customers vs Staff and Profits vs Organizational Health. Thus whilst you would not expect to see conflicts in your Mission Statement it is quite acceptable and, in fact, usually necessary to have built-in conflicts in your Values Statement if it is to be more than just a cute placebo offering little practical help to you when the pressure is really on!

If you look at the Mission and Values in the example project you will see that the goals and objectives of the "Couch to 5K with Fred" project seem to align well. However they also place an important constraint on me that I need to execute these objectives in a way which does not damage my health. In addition there is also a built-in values conflict between my career and my health which I will have to face at some point when my business commitments conflict with my training plans.

STRATEGIC THINKING FOR PLANNING AND EXECUTION
A practical booklet for managers

3. SOCIAL LANDSCAPE

THE KEY QUESTIONS

- Who are the customers?
- Who is investing?
- Who is our team?
- Who are other players?
- Whose help might we need?
- Who might we be in competition with?

PROJECT EXAMPLE: *Couch to 5K with Fred*

Social Landscape Summary

- Mostly for myself (customer)
- My partner wants heathier me (another important customer)
- Friendly competition with Fred (competitive collaboration)
- Doctor/Fitness Coach is a key expert
- Other Park Runners are the competition

PROCESS & TOOLS

ROLE	CHARACTERISTICS
Sponsor/Investors	Main Investor in the project
Strategic Customers	Main beneficiary of project
Operational Customers	Uses the products of the project
Stakeholders	Has a senior interest in the project
Mentor/Coaches	Plays a mentor or coaching role
Champions	Acts as a senior project supporter
Key Influencers	Needs to be on-board with project
Team Members	Essential Team Members
Expert/Advisors	Provides essential expertise
Partners	Collaborates and mutually supports
Suppliers	Assists on a commercial basis
Competitors	Competing against the project

<u>Common Social Landscape Roles</u>

STRATEGIC THINKING FOR PLANNING AND EXECUTION
A practical booklet for managers

A Social Landscape attempts to identify the key people (and if relevant – key groups) on whom the success of the project may depend. It should cover both those who can *help OR hinder* the success of the project (e.g. competitors). The easiest way to construct a Social Landscape is a simple three-column list – name of the person (or group), their main role with respect to the project (see table on the previous page) and how important they could be to its success.

Collaboration and Competition

The second key aspect of a social landscape is exploring the nature of any collaboration and/or competition possibilities. To do this take everybody on your Social Landscape list who is a potential competitor or collaborator and ask two questions:

Question 1: What is the "common ground" where this collaboration or competition would likely occur?

Question 2: What type of competition or collaboration is it?

The diagram below identifies 4 points on a spectrum ranging from *"Pure" Competition* on the right to *"Pure" Collaboration* on the left.

There are two intermediate points - *Competitive (or Edgy) Collaboration* where you are collaborating but with some elements of competition and *Collaborative (or Eco) Competition* where you are competing but with some elements of collaboration. (See my book *"A Systematic Guide to Collaboration and Competition within Organizations"* for more details).

Asking these two questions can identify some important new opportunities with your "competitors" and some potential previously unspoken issues to be carefully managed with your "collaborators".

STRATEGIC THINKING FOR PLANNING AND EXECUTION
A practical booklet for managers

4. INFORMATION RESEARCH

THE KEY QUESTIONS

> - What assumptions are we making?
> - What questions need answered?
> - What conversations need to happen with whom and for what purpose?

PROJECT EXAMPLE: *Couch to 5K with Fred*

> **Information Research Questions**
> - Is this safe for me (Doctor) ?
> - Is there a useful app?
> - Right Gear ?
> - How long?
> - Is Fred committed?

PROCESS & TOOLS

The important thing here is to compile a good list of questions which you need answered to effectively plan your project. This list should cover three main sources of uncertainty:

- Assumptions – how can you confirm or correct these
- Social Landscape (see previous section)
- Unknowns

This list of questions should generate a set of actions which could involve:

- Simple Fact-Finding
- Conversations with Individuals
- Detailed Research or Preparatory work

Another useful tool in the management of uncertainty is **The Knowledge Matrix.**

STRATEGIC THINKING FOR PLANNING AND EXECUTION
A practical booklet for managers

There is a simple 2x2 matrix (see below) we can construct, with post-it notes on a flipchart, to represent the current state of our knowledge of any topic with 4 distinct cells for the purpose of identifying specific clarification actions:

	KNOWN	UNKNOWN
KNOWN	*Known knowns* **Action:** Make sure the whole team know. Check any assumptions.	*Known Unknowns* **Action:** Prioritise and find out.
UNKNOWN	*Unknown Knowns* **Action:** What does someone else in your team know that you all need to know.	*Unknown Unknowns* **Action:** Keep monitoring and be open minded for game changers.

So for example, the cell *Unknown Knowns* (bottom left) identifies important things which one member of you team or network may know which would be very helpful if you also knew! To find this out you need to be willing and able to engage in conversations with your network where you ask, "Is there anything else you think I need to know here?"

STRATEGIC THINKING FOR PLANNING AND EXECUTION
A practical booklet for managers

5. FITNESS ASSESSMENT

THE KEY QUESTIONS

- What does the SWOT Analysis show?
- Sources of Competitive advantage?
- Showstoppers which would make success unlikely?

PROJECT EXAMPLE: *Couch to 5K with Fred*

Fitness Assessment

STRENGTH: I play tennis

WEAKNESS: Bad knees

OPPORTUNITIES: Home Treadmill

THREATS: Frequent Work Travel

Fred works from home – more flexible

If we win new contract in work may need to defer start by 4 weeks

SHOWSTOPPERS

None, subject to Medical Check-up!

PROCESS & TOOLS

The most useful tool here is the good old-fashioned SWOT Analysis (shown overleaf). An important, but often unstated point, about doing an effective SWOT analysis is that it has to be done in the *context* of the proposed project not just in isolation. So what are your strengths and weakness **in terms of making a success of the proposed project**!

Firstly you should examine your Strengths and Opportunities to identify any strengths you can exploit including any sources of potential competitive advantage (assuming there is some element of competition in your project – in our example project – access to a home treadmill).

STRATEGIC THINKING FOR PLANNING AND EXECUTION
A practical booklet for managers

Next you should examine your Weaknesses and Threats to identify if there are any potential **Showstoppers** which should stop you from starting the project as success would be just too unlikely. For example, your medical check-up might result in such a situation.

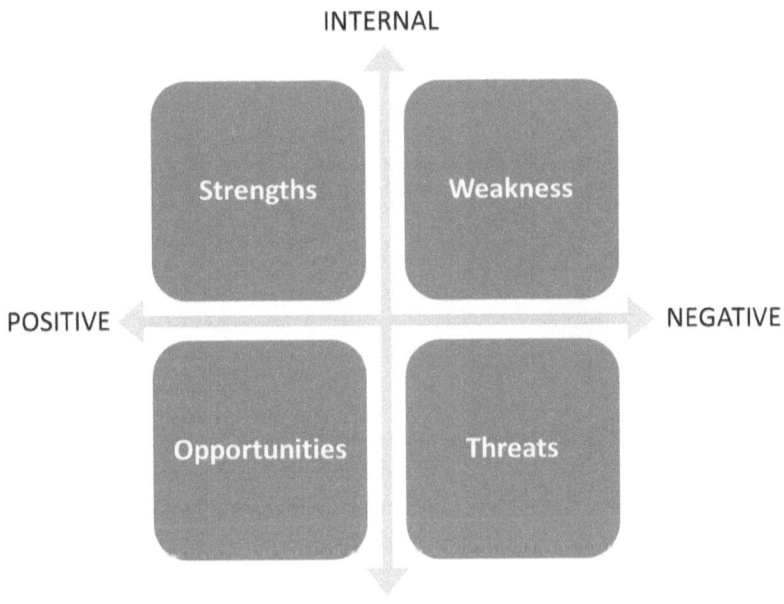

Finally you should then take another look at your Weaknesses and Threats to identify what you can do to mitigate any **Risks** which these present to the proposed project.

For each risk you need to identify three important things:

- **Likelihood** of risk happening (e.g. low, medium or high)
- **Impact** on the project if risk occurred (e.g. low, medium or high)
- **Mitigation** – how you plan to a) reduce likelihood and b) lessen impact

STRATEGIC THINKING FOR PLANNING AND EXECUTION
A practical booklet for managers

6. OBSTACLES & DILEMMAS

THE KEY QUESTIONS

- What obstacles do we expect?
- What dilemmas or trade-offs are likely to be encountered?
- What additional risks does this reveal?

PROJECT EXAMPLE: *Couch to 5K with Fred*

Obstacles
- Pub mates will mock me or interfere with my plans

Dilemmas
- Training when travelling
- Fred too slow or too fast

PROCESS & TOOLS

The first question to ask here is are there any Obstacles or Barriers *which have not yet been identified* which would need to be overcome if this project is to be a success. In the example project my cynical pub mates might give me a hard time or try to make me over indulge in food and drink and damage my fitness.

The second question to ask is about the likely *Dilemmas* I will encounter in the project *which I can anticipate*. Just to be clear, a dilemma is a decision where there is no "pain-free" answer, usually a trade-off between two values. In a sense these dilemmas are special type of risks which might get overlooked in a traditional risk assessment.

There are two good dilemmas in the example project – how will I handle training whilst I am on a business trips and what will I do if it turns out Fred is a much better or much worse runner than me. If these are quite likely to happen then you should think about how you will handle them **in advance** and add them to the *risk mitigation plan* you started to develop in the previous section.

STRATEGIC THINKING FOR PLANNING AND EXECUTION
A practical booklet for managers

7. KEY PERFORMANCE INDICATORS (KPIs)

THE KEY QUESTIONS

- How will success be measured?
- What are the current baseline measures?
- What are the key leading indicators of success?
- What investment will be needed – time and money?
- What are the benefits – qualitative and quantitative?
- What is the Return on Investment?

PROJECT EXAMPLE: *Couch to 5K with Fred*

Success Measures
- Losing 7lbs
- No of 5k runs done

Current Baseline
- Weight: 12 Stone 7 lbs
- Endurance : 0.5 km

Leading Indicators
- Miles per week
- Recovery Heart Rate

Investment:
- Time: 2 hours per week average
- Money: £100 Gear

Benefits
- Feel Good Factor (Qualitative)
- Stamina and Fitness for other activities (Qualitative)
- Avoidance of future health problems

Return on Investment

The value to me of these is much greater than the money and time invested.

STRATEGIC THINKING FOR PLANNING AND EXECUTION
A practical booklet for managers

PROCESS & TOOLS

The questions in this section should not require much clarification other than:

Leading versus Lagging Indicators

Many results, typically financial, happen long after the activity which caused them has ceased. These are referred to as 'lagging' indicators and are outcome measures. They are an essential perspective on a business as ultimately profits are what the business is there to generate. However, because they are lagging indicators they are not effective early warning indicators because by the time you see them all the activities which could have influenced them are over. Example lagging Indicators include Sales, Revenue, Costs and Profits.

Other results, typically non-financial, happen much in advance of the lagging indicators. These are referred to as 'leading' indicators and are activity measures. They are also an essential perspective on a business as they provide excellent early warning systems and can allow you to conduct a Root Cause Analysis of problems. However, because they are leading indicators they are not effective outcome measures and never tell the ultimate story of how a business is doing in a way which would satisfy its investors. Example leading indicators include proposals made per month, exit rates of customers, customer satisfaction levels and employee retention levels.

Return on Investment

There are several different calculations associated with Project Business Cases the main three being:

- **Net Benefits**: the total benefits less the total costs to achieve those benefits.
- **Return on Investment (RoI):** the ratio of the net benefits to the total costs expressed as a percentage.
- **Payback (or Breakeven) Period**: the time taken for the total benefits gained to become equal to the total costs invested.

In some projects it is very difficult to put an number to these benefits but it is still worth trying, even at a broad ballpark level, as it forces you to take some time to try to answer *your most vital question* – **will it be worth all the effort?**

STRATEGIC THINKING FOR PLANNING AND EXECUTION
A practical booklet for managers

8. CRITICAL SUCCESS FACTORS (CSFs)

THE KEY QUESTIONS

- What factors are critical to success?
- Are these factors sufficient collectively?
- Are these factors necessary individually?

PROJECT EXAMPLE: *Couch to 5K with Fred*

Critical Success Factors

1. Medical Check-up
2. Not getting injured
3. Bad Weather Plan
4. Travel Training Plan
5. Gradual Build up of run-times and miles
6. **Expect set-backs and restart**

PROCESS & TOOLS

Critical Success Factors are a really important but much underused tool. The idea is that you identify a list of things which you deem to be **critical** to the success of a project or venture. Then you check your list in two ways:

- Are these factors **sufficient collectively** to achieve the objective?
- Are these factors **necessary individually** to achieve the objective i.e. are there some which are not actually critical?

So at this stage from all your strategic thinking thus far in the previous 7 sections you should have a good list of **potential** Critical Success Factors. You now need to apply these two tests above to this set of factors to come up with a list of factors which are both necessary and sufficient for the success of the project.

For example, in the 5K project I have concluded that once I get started I can still succeed if Fred pulls out or wants to train separately because he is faster or slower than me. Thus this factor is not critical and I have removed it. I also identified that my list was missing a critical factor (being ready for setbacks).

STRATEGIC THINKING FOR PLANNING AND EXECUTION
A practical booklet for managers

9. STRATEGIC SUMMARY

THE KEY QUESTIONS

> - What Options have we considered?
> - What Choices have we made?
> - What Phasing is required?
> - Has the Strategy considered all the Inputs?
> - Does this Articulation help our decision-making and planning?

PROJECT EXAMPLE: *Couch to 5K with Fred*

> **Strategic Summary**
>
> *Options considered but rejected:*
>
> - Get a Fitness Coach
> - Join a running club
> - Lose 7lbs before doing any running
> - Do nothing/Status Quo
>
> Phasing:
>
> - Phase 1: Build to 10 mins in weeks 1-4
> - Phase 2: Build to 20 mins in weeks 5-8
> - Phase 3: Build to 30 mins in weeks 9-12
>
> *Articulation:*
>
> See Single page bullet point summary (page 23) and in particular CSFs section.

PROCESS & TOOLS

The questions in this section do not require much clarification other than to emphasize the importance of Articulation (building on the comments about Agile Stories in the Goals and Objectives Session). One of the biggest problems in organizational projects is the *disconnect* between strategy and implementation – this is known as **The Execution Problem.**

STRATEGIC THINKING FOR PLANNING AND EXECUTION
A practical booklet for managers

There are many reasons for this disconnect but one of the biggest is the failure to summarise your strategy in a succinct enough way to be able to access it when you need to.

When people talk to me about Strategy I often ask them the question:

"How would you know if you had a strategy?"

My answer is you know you have a strategy if there is a simple document, not more than a single page, that you look at when you have a difficult decision or dilemma **and it quickly clarifies what you should do in that moment.**

If your answer is NO then you might have a Strategy Document but not a Strategy!

Your strategy may be supported by many pages of important research and argument but if you cannot find one page somewhere in the document you can use to help you with decision-making then you also will face The Execution Problem.

You can represent your strategy as bullet points or summary narrative or Agile Stories but you must be able to summarise it onto one page as Winston Churchill famously suggested in World War II:

> In 1940, British Prime Minister Winston Churchill sent a memo to his war cabinet stating "To do our work, we all have to read a mass of papers. Nearly all of them are far too long. This wastes time, while energy has to be spent in looking for the essential points. I ask my colleagues and their staff to see to it that their reports are shorter."

STRATEGIC THINKING FOR PLANNING AND EXECUTION
A practical booklet for managers

THE FULL PROCESS ON ONE PAGE

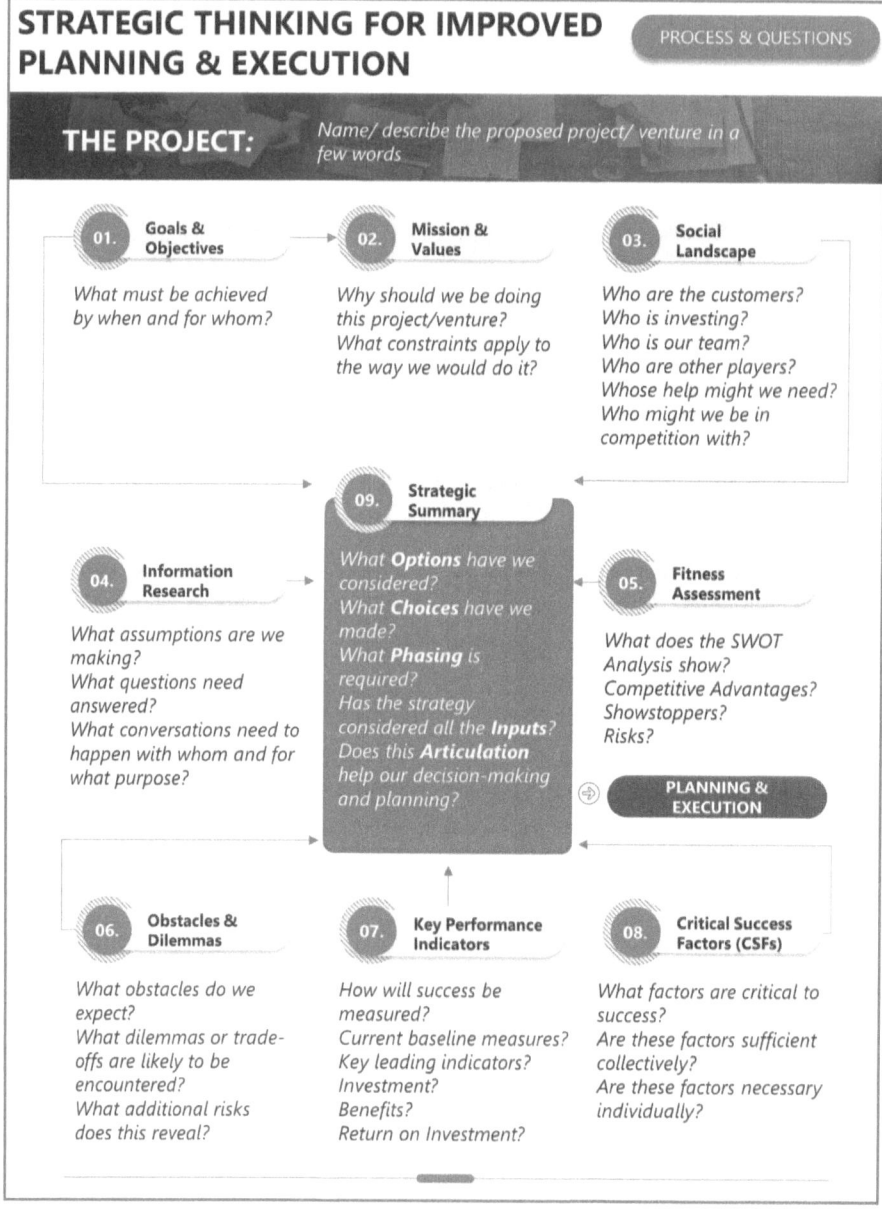

STRATEGIC THINKING FOR PLANNING AND EXECUTION
A practical booklet for managers

WORKED EXAMPLE

STRATEGIC THINKING FOR IMPROVED PLANNING & EXECUTION

PROCESS EXAMPLE

THE PROJECT: Couch to 5K with Fred

 01. Goals & Objectives
- Work up to being able to run 5K with Fred Next Door
- culminating in a Park run in about 3 month's time
- losing half a stone along the way
- whilst doing something a bit competitive
- to improve my health for my own and partners benefit

 02. Mission & Values
- Improve Health (Health)
- Career Development (Business)
- New Hobby (Well-being/Active)
- New Friends (Social)
- Stay Healthy (Safety)

 03. Social Landscape
- Mostly for myself (customer)
- Partner wants heathier me (another customer)
- Friendly competition with Fred (competitive collaboration)
- Doctor/Fitness Coach is a key expert
- Other Park Runners are the competition

 04. Information Research
- Is this safe for me?
- Is there a useful app?
- Right Gear?
- How long?
- Is Fred committed?

09. Strategic Summary

Options considered but rejected:
- Get a Fitness Coach
- Join a running club
- Lose 7lbs before doing any running
- Do nothing/Status Quo

Phasing:
- Phase 1: Build to 10 mins in weeks 1-4
- Phase 2: Build to 20 mins in weeks 5-8
- Phase 3: Build to 30 mins in weeks 9-12

Articulation:
- This Page Suffices

 05. Fitness Assessment
STRENGTH: I play tennis
WEAKNESS: Bad knees
OPPORTUNITIES: Home Treadmill
THREATS: Frequent Work Travel
Fred works from home – flexible
If win new contract in work might need to defer start 1 month
SHOWSTOPPERS
None, subject to Medical Check

 06. Obstacles & Dilemmas

OBSTACLES
- Pub mates will mock me or interfere with my plans

DILEMMAS
- Training when travelling
- Fred too slow or too fast

 07. Key Performance Indicators

SUCCESS MEASURES
- Losing 7lbs
- 5k runs done

BASELINE
- Weight: 12 Stone 7 lbs
- Endurance : 0.5 km

LEADING INDICATORS
- Miles per week
- Recovery Heart Rate

INVESTMENT
- Time: 2 hours/week
- Money: £100 Gear

BENEFITS
- Feel Good Factor
- Stamina and Fitness
- Avoid health problems
ROI – Yes but cant value!

 08. Critical Success Factors (CSFs)
1. Medical Check-up
2. Not getting injured
3. Bad Weather Plan
4. Travel Training Plan
5. Gradual Build up
6. Expect set-backs

STRATEGIC THINKING FOR PLANNING AND EXECUTION
A practical booklet for managers

BLANK TEMPLATE

STRATEGIC THINKING FOR IMPROVED PLANNING & EXECUTION

PROCESS TEMPLATE

THE PROJECT:

01. Goals & Objectives
02. Mission & Values
03. Social Landscape
04. Information Research
05. Fitness Assessment
09. Strategic Summary

STRATEGIC THINKING FOR PLANNING AND EXECUTION
A practical booklet for managers

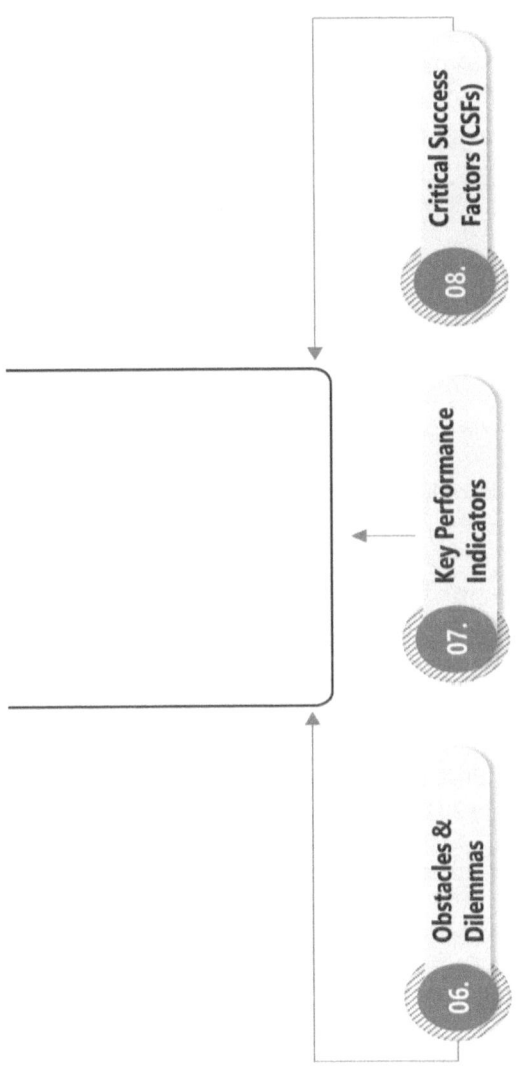

STRATEGIC THINKING FOR PLANNING AND EXECUTION
A practical booklet for managers

THE SYSTEMATIC GUIDES SERIES

The Systematic Guides Series are a collection of comprehensive, practical books each of which outlines the essential skills and practices required for a key management disciplines such as team leadership, business acumen, change management, project management or effective collaboration.

For more details on the concepts introduced in this short booklet please check out the relevant book in the series:

VOLUME 1: A Systematic Guide to High Performing Teams (HPTs), Ken Thompson, December 2015

VOLUME 2: A Systematic Guide to Game-Based Learning (GBL) in Organisational Teams, Ken Thompson, January 2016

VOLUME 3: A Systematic Guide to Business Acumen and Leadership using Dilemmas, Ken Thompson, February 2016

VOLUME 4: A Systematic Guide to Change Management, Ken Thompson, July 2016

VOLUME 5: A Systematic Guide to Collaboration and Competition within Organisations, Ken Thompson, March 2017

VOLUME 6: A Systematic Guide to Project Management, Ken Thompson and Paul Hookham, July 2018

All books are available from <u>Amazon</u> at cost price for training purposes.

STRATEGIC THINKING FOR PLANNING AND EXECUTION
A practical booklet for managers

ABOUT THE AUTHOR

Ken Thompson is an expert practitioner, author and speaker on collaboration, high performing teams, change management, game-based learning, business acumen, strategy, project management, experiential learning and social learning.

Ken's work has featured in major publications including *The Guardian Newspaper, Wired Magazine, The Huffington Post* and *The Henry Ford Magazine*.

Ken has also spoken at many international events including TEDx, the Institute for Healthcare Improvement (IHI), Learn Tech (London) and NASA.

Ken is Managing Director of BusinessSimulations.com and can be contacted via www.businesssimulations.com/.

www.ingramcontent.com/pod-product-compliance
Lightning Source LLC
Chambersburg PA
CBHW031600210526
45464CB00003B/1370